Decoding TRUE Manhood

The 4 Keys to Unlock Your Potential, Passion & Purpose

By Kai Ehnes

"Nothing can bring you peace but yourself. Nothing can bring you peace but the triumph of principles."

~ Ralph Waldo Emerson

---

www.kaiehnes.com

TABLE OF CONTENTS

ACKNOWLEDGMENTS

This book is dedicated to both men and women who are on this quest of self-transformation. This book was conceived with input from both men and women. Men know this new code in their hearts and simply need to remember it and then manifest it. Women want this code actualized in men.

I wish to thank my wife, Tiffany, who has helped me and pushed me to be a better and TRUE man. I thank my mom for a life-long dedication to my well-being. I also want to thank Susanne for doing all of the graphic design for my works.

There have been a tremendous amount of men who have influenced and shaped who I am. I respect and meet each of you where you are. Thank you for guiding me to TRUE manhood.

I wish everyone an exciting journey of self-discovery.

My Why:

"Who in tarnation does this guy think he is, telling us how to be real men?"

I bet that's one of your first thoughts. It surely would be mine. Well, I don't pretend to know anything that makes me superior. I come to you as a fellow traveler. Much of what I was told as a boy about masculinity turns out to be false, and misleading . . . even damaging to the psyche of the modern man.

I have been on a quest throughout my life to uncover and decode the Truth about what it means to truly be a man. My discoveries have shown me that there are Keys to being a better man, and now I'd like to share these insights with you.

With these Keys an actualized man gets to unlock doors. These doors are the proverbial layers one has to peel away to get to the ultimate Truth. This is what I have to offer to myself and to you. As each one of us finds our true purpose, the feeling of being lost or disconnected will gradually disappear. By doing this work, there will be a ripple effect will be endless.

This is why I am so passionate about helping other men to ignite their collective lifting of male consciousness. Everyone will benefit. The true purpose for life.

WHO AM I?

I was born in the 1960s, in a country that used to be called West Germany. My biological father was barely around when I was little. He was a police officer and fundamentally believed that people were inherently evil and needed to be *"straightened out"* and *"tuned up."* He was a man who used alcohol, tobacco, and women to fulfill his shortcomings. He inadvertently taught me about the abuse of patriarchy and the dark, shadow side of unbalanced masculinity. He raised me with fear and a heavy hand but my mother fared much worse.

When I was eight, my mother decided that she had tolerated enough abuse and divorced my father, which at the time was scandalous for women in our small German village. She maintained custody of me and my father received limited visitation rights.

On one visit he arrived drunk and was shouting furiously at my mother. He decided that if he couldn't have her, then no one could, as he pulled out his service revolver and threatened to take her life. I was only nine years old as I watched the drama unfold right in front of me. I decided right then that this was not the way for a true man to behave. I walked up to my inebriated and angry father and took the gun from him.

Soon after that incident, my mother remarried an American Military Officer. By the time I was sixteen, my step-father was stationed back in the United States and he took his new family with him.

So I learned to speak English and began my new life in America. In those days there were no programs to help with that transition so I had to learn English in two months in order to function in school. I also had to adjust to an entirely new culture. I will say that to this day, I enjoy being a German immigrant in America. Now that I am a citizen of this great country, I have been able to adopt the best of both worlds into my way of being.

My new "father" took on the role of financial provider (a task that he did well), but he did not understand how to model manhood either. When he was around, my step-father demonstrated different qualities of the shadow side of masculinity. He was distant, cold, numb, and detached--as if something dark had happened to him a long time ago in boyhood and he could never let it go and move on.

Up to that point I was basically an appendage of my mother. She had me in tow through most of her experiences and subsequent decisions. So while I had two fathers, I was actually raised and programmed by my mother and her female friends. Specifically, these women established my viewpoint on men—whom they viewed as either weak or highly abusive.

Whenever I asserted my masculinity, I was told that I was too assertive, too strong or too big. I was told by the female guard to "*turn it down*," or "*don't be so hard*!" I can't tell you how often I heard that message conveyed both covertly and overtly through the women around me.

There was a definite absence of positive male role models to be my guide. As an only child, I had no brothers, and my uncles were back in Germany. Within this vacuum of male guidance, I had to learn to fend for myself.

And so my journey began. By the age of seventeen, I was questioning the qualities of what an authentic, true man was supposed to be. I yearned to understand why so many adult men that I encountered seemed to be missing these qualities. I wanted to know.

I did notice that a few of the boys were guided by their fathers; not just disciplined and ridiculed into submission--but actually advised, instructed, and chaperoned through the tough sea of adolescence. These fathers instilled a sense of worthiness into their sons as they advised and shepherded—showing the next generation of young men the pathway to manhood. But this breed of father seemed rare and I wondered why.

Then, in my senior year of high school, my English teacher had us study about King Arthur and the Noble Knights. I learned about the Knight's Code and their virtues . . . finding myself completely hooked. Symbolism and deep philosophical insights . . . I was at home. These were real men. A community of brothers with a virtuous code to live by, and a higher purpose to guide them. These men believed in something greater than themselves. I instantly knew I wanted to be part of a brotherhood of authentic men.

What I couldn't understand is that the other young men around me had no desire for a code to live by. I listened and watched and found their lack of brotherhood very distressing. Again, I had to make this journey on my own. I continued this quest for knowledge in college, seeking the truth about virtues from philosophy, books, and my professors.

The good news is that growing up with an absence of balanced masculine energy left me hungry to research and learn for myself. I had the prime opportunity to decide what makes an authentic man by my own volition. I pushed myself to be better and live more virtuously. I succeeded most of the time. Where I failed, I had room to grow.

Now I am a father of two young men, who are finding their own path into adulthood. My own father has passed away and my step-father is feeling his age. I am the bridge between three generations of men, who all seek healing, truth and purpose in their own way. It appears that we are all searching for that sense of brotherhood and connection with like-minded men

WHAT IS TRUE ABOUT MANHOOD?

TRUE Manhood is an age-old theory dating back to ancient cultures such as the Greeks, the Celts, and the Druids. Yet psychology, sociology, history and anthropology have shown us that what we consider to be "masculinity" has really been the dark side of "patriarchy." While our modern culture often uses these two terms interchangeably, they are most definitely not the same thing.

Here is a standard dictionary definition of each:

MASCULINITY:

Having qualities traditionally ascribed to men, such as strength and boldness.

PATRIARCHY:

A social system in which power is held by men, through cultural norms and customs that favor men and withhold opportunities from women.

Up until now, western culture has been fixated in patriarchal adolescence. No matter our chronological age, most men still react from a young boy's perspective . . . our ego and pride is easily wounded, our reactions are either boyish tantrums of frustration or endless hours of sullen pouting. As Robert Bly suggests in his book *Iron John,* without rituals or initiation into manhood, our childhood has been prolonged, and our only concept of brotherhood is a college fraternity. Even our modern corporations are ruled by patriarchy and the *"boys' network."*

We have not been allowed to become men . . . but have remained Man-Boys far into adulthood. We physically look like grown-ups, but we have not grown up at all. There have been too few older men or mentors to show most of us how.

With the women's rights and feminist movements, men were told to access their feminine side, yet still remain strong, yet gentle, yet bold, but share the power, yet take the lead . . . and men became very confused. In fact, this system has been off balance for men as far back as the Industrial Revolution (*but that's a history lesson for another day*).

While asking men to access their feminine side has some merit, women don't really want a feminized man for the long haul. It's also not socially or psychologically healthy for either gender to remain cut off from the truth of who they are, nor is it good for our family structures or our communities.

But after my fifty years of life research, I have witnessed and experienced that there is another level of masculinity for men to explore that can provide better balance and support for themselves and their feminine counterparts. Some call this next level the Divine Masculine, or the Authentic Masculine. I call it TRUE Manhood.

So what does this new step in masculine evolution even look like? These are men who are balanced in their yin and yang energy, and live their life with passion and purpose. We shall call this class of men the Noble Knights. And what do these men do differently than the rest of us that are caught up in the culture we were raised in? That is what we will uncover together through this process.

Just like the Noble Knights of olden days, they live by a code--a set of principles so pure that they embody the spirit and world-views expressed in all great manifestations. Similar codes were proposed by the Founding Fathers of the United States, and the European Age of Enlightenment.

Many of these principles will be explained in greater detail in my upcoming book—***The 12 Doors to Unlocking Manhood***. But we can lay out the basic concepts here, because we will need the right KEYS before we can open any doors.

THE FOUR KEYS TO TRUE MANHOOD

These Keys are summarized by the term TRUE!

T = TRUTHFUL

R = ROOTED

U = UNDERSTANDING OUR CONNECTION

E = ENLIGHTENED SELF-INTEREST

KEY #1: T which stands for **Truthful**

KEY #2: R which stands for **Rooted**

KEY #3: U which stands for Understanding our Connection

KEY #4: E which stands for **Enlightened Self-Interest**

These Keys will show how an actualized adult man learns to be accurate and appropriate in his ways. His decisions are based on intuitively knowing what to do. This TRUE man will be authentic, which means to be genuine, honest and sincere in his interactions with himself and others, as well as the community, and the planet. This is our natural way of being. All young boys (and girls as well) are innately born with these Keys until society and culture twist us out of our natural alignment.

Once a man has become comfortable in his own skin, he will be back in balance with life. He will be stalwart and reliable. He will be compassionate and heart-centered. The Keys to being a TRUE man will unlock all of these qualities. Imagine being that which you have always known but have suppressed for the sake of paychecks and trophies.

KEY 1 – TRUTHFUL

Let's briefly examine some of the definitions of what it means to be truthful.

- Be honest with yourself. A man must first be truthful with himself before he can learn to be truthful with others.

- Speak honestly to others about your truth; do not pretend to be something that you're not. This means that you must take off your social mask and be the genuine and natural you—not the version of you that society or culture wants you to be.

- Honesty is speaking the truth, but it is also in your actions and behavior. Behave in ways that honor your truth. Be authentic in your actions. You honor yourself when you *walk your talk*." This means to be honorable in your thoughts, words, and deeds— being truthful entails following through on what you say you will do.

- A man must learn to be consistent in his actions. When you are known to be credible and your word is reliable, you will get further in your life with other men, women, friends, family, community, and business.

- Take care not to speak words about others that are untrue. You are not being honest if you pass on rumors about someone. A brotherhood of good men is built on trust but that bond is delicate and can be broken with a whisper. Before you speak, ask yourself, *"Is this true? Is this helpful? Is this inspiring? Is this necessary? Is this kind?"*

- Be in alignment with your own code of virtues and moral compass. Being honest means you admit to your actions, even if you might get into trouble. If you do cross a line, don't attempt to deny, lie or hide, but sincerely admit what you have done with open candor. The next step would be to make actual amends (but speaking the truth is the first step).

Many of us grew up in a house where speaking the truth was discouraged or even downright dangerous. For example, would it be safe to tell your father the truth if you didn't want to take over the family business? Were you given the chance to choose from any major in college or was one path already chosen for you? Were you allowed to make choices that were different from the socially accepted status quo of what was expected for you?

As young boys, how often were we told to hide our true feelings with messages such as *"boys don't cry,"* or *"don't be a sissy."* I can recall kissing my father on the cheek when I was two--just to show him how much I loved him. He smacked me hard across the face and told me never to do that again. *"Men don't ever show love,"* was the message that I received that day.

If we were not allowed to feel and express ourselves as children, then how are we supposed to know what we are feeling as adults. How many adult men react with anger and frustration when what they are truly feeling is hurt or scared? We may have learned to react big when we feel small, or we may have learned to go numb inside, disconnect

ACTIVITIES

I have two activities to help you with this process.

At the end of this eBook, you will find an activity where you can **Make Your Own Code**. This process will help you clarify who you truly are and what you truly want from your life.

I also have a **FREE Action Guide** for working through each category of your life and the level of fulfillment that you feel. I would be delighted to send this Action Guide to you. For this FREE guide, simply email me at: kai@kaiehnes.com.

our emotional limbic system, and throw our efforts into the job. It feels safer that way.

That is why the first Key to unlocking authentic manhood requires us to identify our own Truth. You cannot be honest with anyone else until you are honest with yourself. Sometimes being honest with yourself is the hardest part. Men have been so conditioned to go to work, pay the bills, and support the family. We stay so busy and distracted by our modern life that we don't have time for seeking the Truth.

Who are you? What do you want to do with your life?

What are you most passionate about? What do you love to do?

Who would you be if you had all the freedom in the world (which by the way, you do)?

For more on how to unlock your Truth, email me (kai@kaiehnes.com) for my **FREE Action Guide** or visit my web site (www.kaiehnes.com).

Socrates also agreed with this sentiment as he stated *"An unexamined life is not worth living"* (as quoted in Plato's Republic). We have stopped asking ourselves the two most essential questions of our daily existence:

How do I feel?

What do I want?

As you pause for a moment and consider those questions, try to dig deeper than the simple, short-term answers . . . *"I want a cold beer," "I want a raise," "I want a new car,"* and so on. Why not sit with these questions on a deeper, soulful level?

HOW DO I FEEL?

Right here, right now, in this very moment, how do you feel about your life, your work, your decisions, your family, and your partnerships? What if you could actually admit out loud how you feel and unburden yourself of all of the things that you have never admitted to anyone else before? You don't need to say these things to anyone else but yourself. It starts with being honest with you.

WHAT DO I WANT?

What do you hear your soul calling you to do? If the word "*soul*" doesn't work for you, find another word. What possibilities did you hope for as a child? What do you wish you could do in the next year, or the next five years? What are you yearning to do in retirement? What if you could start the soul's calling right now with one small step in the direction of your dreams?

HELP

If something that you need to speak about is too awful to deal with, then reach out and get help. Part of this transition to the next level of manhood is to develop a brotherhood that you can depend on. In tribal days, there would have been a circle of wise elders you could have gone to. Today we have specialists, counselors, and support groups that can help.

KEEPING IT REAL

Once you have been honest with yourself, it is time to speak the Truth to others. An authentic man uses his words wisely, and speaks responsibly. Be sure that what you say is factual and verifiable—this will actually help you to feel more confident and your words will carry more authority. Bragging that you had four business sales doesn't need to be inflated to six just so that you can look better socially. Saying what you think the crowd wants to hear versus reality will actually cost you in your credibility. Take an honest inventory of yourself and the stories you are telling. Watch the words that are leaving your lips. Are you walking your talk in every area of your life?

To be honest also means to be free of fraud. Truthfulness requires you to be fair in dealing with others . . . in business, in the community, and at home. Our interactions with others must be straightforward and honorable . . . never deceptive or misleading. A man of integrity does not cheat his fellow man. The current movement towards conscious capitalism and a sustainable business mindset is an example of this Truthfulness.

Consider all of the online storing of information, and then compound that with the security breaches of data. People's lives are becoming more and more transparent. Lying and dishonesty cannot be sustained for long. Attempting to keep the Truth from coming out is exhausting and physically damaging to your body, mind and spirit.

THINK BEFORE YOU SPEAK

So what I am asking you to do is to join me in stripping away the years of lies and pretending, and just tell it like it is. This doesn't mean you have the right to be cruel and unleash every random thought that comes into your head with no restraint. Many people misuse the concept of "*speaking the truth*" to verbally eviscerate someone in their life. The need to "*speak the truth*" does not trump common decency of compassion, kindness and appropriate timing.

There is a way to say the Truth directly but with tact, to refrain from being hurtful. We can learn to practice restraint when selecting our words. Truth is meant to be a tool for healing . . . not a weapon. Be cautious that your truth serum does not become tainted with poison. Speaking our Truth is a gift, and sharing our Truth can be a healing antidote to pain. This vulnerable giving of our truest self should be done with care and compassion for all involved.

Before you speak, stop and use the acronym THINK. Ask yourself:

T = Is this True?

H = Is this Helpful?

I = Is this Inspiring?

N = Is this Necessary?

K = Is this Kind?"

KEY 2 – ROOTED

In the Chinese culture the word *"dantien"* refers to the space just below your navel where your grounded, earthy energy and power comes from. For the modern man, we tend to be cut off from that power within our bodies (unless you have practiced Tai Chi or one of the martial arts). The corporate life requires men to live in their heads, disconnected and cut off from any anything lower than the neck (except for the groin area). So we are walking, talking heads with groins. Everyday, we are making decisions from this cut-off, numbed out, disconnected place.

Part of what the *"new"* man must learn to do is to ground himself into that *dantien* region of the body. This is what Sam Keen spoke about with his men's book *Fire in the Belly*. This is the region where a man's true passion and genuine life force comes from.

The next step in our evolution, will be to pull that *dantien* energy up the body to reconnect with the heart and chest area. The broadest area on most men is their shoulders and chest region, yet we avoid tapping into that part of the body because it involves the heart and emotions.

The heart is the last place that modern men are taught to explore. We will travel into space, to the bottom of the ocean floor, the top of a mountain top, or even into an active volcano before we will open ourselves up to the vulnerability that lives in the heart. We are so afraid of being hurt—but not being Truthful to ourselves hurts so much more. We must learn that there is a way to safely feel all of our passion and still be balanced as men.

This Key is all about knowing who you are. Consider how beautiful it is to be that MAN who exudes the right energy because he knows himself. Others are instantly aware of this quality. This man is grounded. He is calm and assertive in his dealings with himself and the world. This is best represented by the archetype of the balanced Buddhist monk or Zen master.

I am not saying that you have to become a Buddhist monk, or meditate 3 hours a day . . . but rather that a real man possesses these types of qualities:

- These men allow time each day for self-reflection on their thoughts and actions.

- They spend the time it takes to work through any shadow issues to become a clean slate. Only a wound that is clean can heal. A wound that has not been cleaned will develop gangrene and fester.

- These men learn to see the world from a clean perspective, and to release judgment or jealousy of others. As the Dalai Lama explains when defining love; *"love is the absence of judgment."*

- They do not brag or boast about their accomplishments, but instead reflect their true selves in a way that is both vulnerable and powerful simultaneously.

- Many monks understand the martial arts, and they carry a great power which they may never need to use. To have that power, and not use it, is a sign of true inner strength.

- Part of their daily life is to do chores which they do with mindfulness and gratitude rather than the western way of completing our responsibilities through frustration and resentment.

- These men live in a brotherhood of kindness and compassion, in which they learn unity and sharing.

A rooted man is strong . . . emotionally, physically, and spiritually. He carries the energy of a Zen master. Nothing waivers this energy. He can rock back into his own *dantien* energy whenever he needs to and resettle himself.

A rooted man is settled in his mind and in his heart because he has mastered Key #1: Truthfulness. He knows himself and has been honest with himself and those he cares about. All of our sporadic decision-making, addictions, escapism, and fight-or-flight behavior occur when we have not become rooted in our own truth. When we take inventory of ourselves at the deepest levels, and face whatever is lurking in the shadows, we become more rooted with each step along the way.

Rooted also means that the man is open to developing ties to those close to him . . . his family, his spouse, his community, and his brotherhood of men. He is connected to the environment, and he finds comfort in nature. In turn, nature finds comfort in him. He becomes a steward of the earth and nature. He senses the interconnectedness between himself and the ecosystem that he is part of. By knowing his place, a rooted man takes full responsibility for himself and his place in time.

"Always in the big woods when you leave familiar ground and step off alone into a new place there will be, along with the feelings of curiosity and excitement, a little nagging of dread. It is the ancient fear of the Unknown, and it is your first bond with the wilderness you are going into. You are undertaking the first experience, not of the place, but of yourself in that place. It is an experience of our essential loneliness, for nobody can discover the world for anybody else. It is only after we have discovered it for ourselves that it becomes a common ground and a common bond, and we cease to be alone."

~ Wendell Berry

Part of this stalwart man's awareness is the understanding of the balance between long-term and short-term thinking, which I teach as having a Sustainable Mindset. When faced with making decisions he has trained himself to know that short-term decisions must be balanced with the desired long-term results. This balance must be applied to all areas of our life including business and family life.

The extremes of this duality would be a man who only acts in the now (short-term) for the sake of instant gratification, while the other extreme is someone who does not act at all because of the possibility of making a mistake. The balanced man is fully aware of the long-term implications while still being able to act in the now. Men are forward-moving and forward-thinking in our very nature so we need this ability to hunt new ideas, and act on new impulses, but we must temper that adventurous desire with the long-run consequences of our decisions.

An example of this is the Law of Seven Generations from the Iroquois nation which tells us to think 140 years into the future when deciding whether the decisions we make today will benefit our children seven generations into the future.

What if we all considered this filter of thinking when deciding on buying the cheapest good possible that is made out of plastic versus the biodegradable version that helps to foster a healthy ecosystem? Or do we grow the cheapest form of immediate quick food versus a sustainable rotation of crops that helps nourish the soil?

A rooted man trains himself to internalize this filter so that decisions are made within

LOOKING AHEAD

"We are looking ahead , as is one of the first mandates given us as chiefs, to make sure and to make every decision that we make relate to the welfare and well-being of the seventh generation to come...." "What about the seventh generation? Where are you taking them? What will they have?" Oren Lyons, Chief of the Onondaga Nation this context. This is known as having a Sustainable Mindset. This is the basis for the conscious business movement which seeks to raise corporate awareness and implement practices that will benefit both human beings and the environment. This awareness is spreading into corporate social responsibility in the community, as well as socially responsible investing, and conscious consumerism. Just as all roads lead to Rome, so should all of our decisions lead back to the law of Seven Generations.

Imagine for a moment how a community or brotherhood of real men would function. Men would be Truthful (Key 1) and Rooted (Key 2). You would know that the men you interact with for business and commerce transactions are practicing these similar qualities. The childish games of one upmanship and competition for the sake of winning would simply fade away. It is boyhood behavior anyway, and not the behavior of adult men.

On top of that, envision your legacy—what you will leave behind after you are gone. All the wealth in the world cannot go with us when we depart. The only lasting impact of our lives is truly how we interact with others and the world around us. If we made solid, compassionate decisions, then our legacy would support and nurture those we love for seven generations and beyond. If you were to die today, your slate would be clean, and your legacy would live on, because your daily decisions and actions are Rooted and Truthful.

KEY 3 – UNDERSTANDING OUR CONNECTION

UNDERSTANDING: A state of mutually cooperative relations between people through enlightened intelligence **and empathy**

Now that you have taken some time to learn your own Truth, and to become rooted in that Truth, it is time to understand your connection to the greater good.

What is your WHY?

Why are you here? Why do you do what you do?

What are you passionate about?

What is your higher calling or purpose?

How can you be of service to others?

Key #3 is about unlocking the greater WHY that lies dormant within all of us. We can make all the money in the world, or be the most successful person we know, but if a man is not asking about his greater WHY, he is still playing small. This is what Marianne Williamson was referring to when she wrote, *"Your playing small does not serve the world." (A Return to Love).*

If we do not challenge ourselves with this greater understanding of our place in the universe, then our lives will remain stunted, and stagnant, and our 'greatest gifts' will remain hidden from ourselves and those around us. This is what Henry David Thoreau meant when he wrote, *"Most men lead **lives of quiet desperation** and go to the grave with the song still in them."*

Our role as TRUE men is to learn how to serve not only ourselves and our families but also how we can better serve the world. In understanding yourself you will see your connection to your community. There will be a place for you to help and guide others.

Young boys will also want to follow your lead and become TRUE men. Without real men as role models it makes sense why our young boys have chosen a life of video games and shallow relationships. They change majors and jobs as fast as they upgrade technology. Happiness must be at the next job or in the next relationship or even at the next level of the game. Our young men believe that the answers they seek are to be found in external validation and instant material gratification. There must be a start over button when they don't like the way the game is going.

Most of our young men today are not rooted . . . but how could they be if their fathers were not rooted, and their fathers before them? Who is going to teach us how to be grounded and stalwart in our life? For a long time I was a single father with two small boys and I remember how our seasons were not determined by the cycles of nature but by which sporting event I was car-pooling them to and from. There was soccer season, and karate season, baseball and football season, and we rushed to get to each one.

It wasn't until I moved out of the suburbs and into the country that I learned what the seasons of life were really for. As I became a gentlemen farmer for our modest croft I had to re-learn the rhythms of nature. I had lost touch with the time to harvest, plant, grow, reap, sow, rest, and so on. As I reclaimed the land, the land reclaimed me and my soul became more rooted and grounded in the natural process.

As we grow and transform into TRUE men, we will be able to offer better guidance and assistance to the younger generations. But you cannot teach what you do not know, so first we must heal ourselves before we can guide others.

Men have lived in a constant state of adolescence for centuries. We have been held back as boys even as we physically mature into an adult man's body. Psychologically, many of us have remained Man-Boys, still stifled in our emotional and personal growth. We live out boyhood games through fraternities and other adolescent diversions. This mentality then evolves into "boys clubs" in our corporations, communities, and politics.

But when do we actually make the transition and transform into adulthood? Without mentors, or initiations into manhood, how does the boy know that he has become a man? No one gives us a guide book or a map that shows us how to get there. In the western world, we have created false goal posts to cross—the first drink of alcohol, turning 21 and partying until you puke, your first sexual experience, fast cars, getting married, having a child, owning a home, etc. We do all of these things because we think they will make us into men.

When did you think you became a man?

Someone forgot to mention that partying until you puke is not the pinnacle of what real manhood is about. Nor is taking on mountains of responsibility and debt just to keep up appearances of maturity. For example: first experience with money at eighteen our children sign student loans that equal house prices, yet they have barely held minimum wage jobs.

Our old systems have been based on boyish thinking and adolescent bullying. The petty rules of patriarchy that we have been following have hurt our communities, our businesses, and our families. The old rules of greed and corruption are oppressive to most, and have kept our society stagnant. Boys grab and hoard; men share and unite. TRUE men nurture, uplift, and expand.

TRUE men must move beyond boyhood games and pre-set social patterns. We must develop a mature sense of belonging and connectedness to ourselves, to others, and to the planet. The third Key is about how we connect what we learn as leaders in our family, business, and communities. Once we are *Rooted* and *Truthful*, we can now make a larger impact on the world.

Part of *Understanding our Connection* to others is about learning *empathy* which means to care for the thoughts, feelings, and attitudes of another. It is a different concept than having *sympathy* for someone, although sympathy is often a good place to start.

SYMPATHY *is acknowledging another person's emotional hardships and providing assurance, but it is from an outside perspective. It separates the person who is in pain from the person who is outside the pain.*

EMPATHY *is knowing how someone else feels because you have the same capacity within yourself. It is a deeper understanding of compassion and unconditional love.*

TRUE men have a well refined sense of empathy and learn to exude this love in all areas of their lives.

TRUE men learn to align with nature and live within the boundaries of the system's carrying capacity. They become stewards of animals and plants, as well as the water and earth . . . not just as natural resources, but as part of a greater interconnected ecosystem.

KEY 4 – ENLIGHTENED SELF-INTEREST

"Do well by doing good."

This phrase is often credited to Benjamin Franklin who offers a great example of a man who understands the ethical and philosophical concept of enlightened self-interest. Whether this self-interest is expressed through an individual, group, or business, the concept basically states that we ultimately serve our own self-interest even as we serve others.

Franklin was an early thought leader in today's movement towards corporate social responsibility. Good old Ben demonstrated how to be a successful entrepreneur and still have compassion for the greater good. Franklin was wealthy enough to retire in his early 40's and became one of the wealthiest men of his time, yet the money was never what Franklin based his success on.

He firmly believed that it was every man's civic responsibility to contribute to society, and that through this connection, a man would live the *'good life.'* Franklin once stated that he would rather have people remember that he *"lived usefully,"* than to remember that he *"died rich."* Franklin continued to pursue civic projects and carry out benevolent acts throughout the rest of his life . . . from creating hospitals and firehouses to universities.

Many of our original founding fathers accepted this concept into their definition of manhood and they used this idea when creating the early documents for the United States. Enlightened self-interest was also of great interest to the thought leaders of the Enlightenment in Europe, including a well-known economist by the name of Adam Smith.

Adam Smith wrote about enlightened self-interest in his book, The Wealth of Nations. He explained that "It is not from the benevolence of the butcher, the brewer, or the baker, that we expect our dinner, but from their regard to their own interest. We address ourselves, not to their humanity but to their **self-love**, and never talk to them of our necessities but of their advantages." Smith adds on, "By pursuing his own interest, he frequently promotes that of the society more effectually."

In other words, people will pursue their own self-interest which is an inherent aspect of being human. But, Smith explains, we do not have to pursue only a narrow short-run view. The quick, easy, selfish way only leads to greed and imbalance in ourselves, our families, and our communities.

Smith's writings clarify that there is also a fundamental nature of people to care about others and accept the responsibilities of humanity outside of just ourselves. This involves long-term planning and thinking that moves beyond our own selfish needs.

Smith's theories have provided the foundation of our contemporary economic wisdom – yet we have misunderstood much of what he was trying to convey. By pursuing our own self-care and self-interest, we can also transform our personal achievements into something of greater value for the public. Sometimes the greatest societal good can come from the greatest individual self-interest.

As men, we have been taught to become leaders in our communities and captains of industry, yet no one has guided us how to do this in an enlightened way. The economy of greed is not the goal we should be aiming for. The sign of a TRUE man and a Good King to lead will be an economy of enlightenment which values compassion, relationships, and ethics as well as the individual.

Often Key #4 makes more sense by looking at its opposite . . . *unenlightened self-interest*, or in simple terms . . . greed. Most of us would agree that when men act out of their own myopic selfishness, the group as a whole suffers as a result. This breakdown creates dis-ease at the systemic level in any corporation or community and leads to conflict, miscommunication, discontent, and a general lack of cooperation.

In today's world our dominant paradigm is that money equals success and success means more life. The players who adopt this way of thinking accumulate money in the hopes of securing more life for themselves.

Systems that are created through *unenlightened self-interest* are built upon the concept of scarcity. This means that there is limitation everywhere, which in turn creates competition for those resources available. With everyone vying for a few limited resources anything becomes fair game, and all of life becomes a battlefield to be conquered.

Modern corporations have made profits the most important goal. The actual people that they are supposed to serve have become marginalized, and so has the environment that these businesses need to survive. Profits have become more important than people, or even the planet, yet without those last two items, the profits will not last.

We know that building any foundation on this inefficient patriarchal hierarchy only leads to each individual paying a higher price for the protection of their own interests, yet we have continued to create a system that puts profits over people in all areas. While some individuals might temporarily profit from a philosophy of greed, we see from history that it is not a system of thinking that can be sustained beyond one generation. It definitely fails the Seven Generations test as mentioned earlier.

The time has passed for petty bickering about who is on the left or the right politically. It is time to find your center in all things . . . emotionally balanced and ethically rooted in your Truth. A community of TRUE men will build mature, long-range policies and economic sustainability for the community in which every member can thrive.

In the wise words of Adam Smith, *"A nation is not made wealthy by the childish accumulation of shiny metals, but it enriched by the economic prosperity of its people."*

So by contrast, ***enlightened self-interest*** is humanitarian, charitable, and idealistic while simultaneously being utilitarian – useful, beneficial and practical. Merging an enlightened attitude with self-interest brings a whole new level of efficiency to our own lives as well as to society.

It is related to the Golden Rule which states that we should act toward others the way we would want them to act toward us. This does not mean that everyone we meet will be reciprocal in our kindness, but I have noticed that all of my good deeds do come back to me through the kindness of others in a *"pay it forward"* sort of way. In this regard, each man creates the type of society that he would like to be a part of . . . whether it be *"honor among thieves"* or a brotherhood of Noble Knights. We do indeed reap what we sow.

Enlightened self-interest also involves delayed gratification and making long-run decisions that will pass the Seven Generations test. When we are petty and selfish, we tend to make poor short-term decisions that we will later regret. Think of the money, resources, and time we waste when decisions are only made with the short-run goal in mind. While long-term benefits may require temporary sacrifice, they will result in positive long-term outcomes that are overall better for the greater whole.

Here is a simple example of this concept . . . Imagine a small store that refuses to accept a return on an item. They have made a short-term gain but have lost the customer forever, as well as any future profits from word of mouth recommendations. How many future, long-term sales will the store lose now that they have lost their reputation for being reasonable to buy from? Think about the last time you suffered from poor customer service with a company. Would you buy from them again? Has that experience created a negative imprint in your memories that has altered where you shop?

That is the difference between *selfishness* and *enlightened self-interest*. Selfishness put a couple of extra dollars in your pocket but lost you long-term relationships with customers that could have brought you thousands of dollars more. In all of our dealings with the world, it is better to build relationships that last, and policies that create a healthy longevity with the community you serve. This in turn creates a flow of good will ever coming your way.

"Enlightened self-interest," as explained by Alexander de Tocqueville, *"holds that people voluntarily join together in associations to further the interests of the group and, thereby, serve their own interests."*

What could *enlightened self-interest* look like in politics and in our communities? In 1972, the country of Bhutan began working with a concept called **Gross National Happiness** (GNH). The phrase is used to express a commitment to building an economy that would serve Bhutan's culture based on Buddhist spiritual values instead of the western material development that is represented by gross domestic product (GDP). The four pillars of GNH philosophy are:

Sustainable development

Preservation and promotion of cultural values

Conservation of the natural environment

Establishment of good governance

The GNH concept has inspired a modern political happiness movement that has spread throughout the world. In 2007, Thailand released the Green and Happiness Index (GHI). South Korea, Goa (India), Singapore, Dubai, the United Kingdom, and even Seattle (Washington) have launched similar happiness indexes. In 2011, the United Nations placed "happiness" on the global development agenda.

Often *enlightened self-interest* is confused with the concept of *altruism*, but these two concepts are subtly different.

> ***Altruism*** *states that people should act in the interest of others often at the expense of their own interests and with no expectation of benefit for themselves in the future.*
>
> ***Enlightened Self-Interest*** *states that in serving others we will directly or indirectly be servicing ourselves. Enlightened self-interest lets the individual meet their own needs.*

Both concepts generally come from good intentions but the outcomes of altruism might not always be good for humanity, and often lead to inefficiency. Without understanding our greater objective purpose for the common good (Key #3) our actions can be kind and charitable, yet remain unenlightened . . . often with unintended consequences.

Enlightened self-interest is also a great system of checks and balances. Society needs to balance the far-sighted planner with the near-sighted doer. In this way, we make decisions and take action but now it is within the framework of continuity and sustainability.

How will this play out within the context of being a real man? Here is the formula:

1. Take inventory of your self-interests

2. Take stock of the needs of the group (which could be your family, your town, your business)

3. Practice emanating the good-will you want for yourself to the group first, then the group in turn will provide the good will to you.

In general, human beings are primarily interested in their own welfare. Psychologist Hans Selye stated that humans strive to achieve and maintain happiness. This basic need is the most ancient and important impulse that motivates all human beings. At the same time humans also possess social interest. We wish to ensure that the social system as a whole survives and simultaneously evolves.

In summary, humans strive for self-interest, as well as, the desire to promote social interest for others. A TRUE man promulgates a long list of life principles that will benefit the group--agape, love, charity, affection, altruism, amity, attachment, humanity, tender heart, goodwill goodness, generosity, clemency, kind, grace, charity, benevolence . . . the list goes on and on.

Consider for a moment what life led by these principles would be like for your community? Now the path to TRUE Manhood emerges. *Enlightened self-interest* will make a brotherhood, promote fellowship, kinship, and create a community of men which will elevate the entire community.

IN CONCLUSION

Think of it like the legendary Knights of the Roundtable. Each Knight brought their own experience, desires, passion and self-interest, yet each Knight also lived and fought for the Noble ideals of the Roundtable. The virtues and ideals of the Roundtable gave the Knight the higher purpose that allowed each Knight to create meaning in their lives. Now, I realize this is a fictional archetype of what a utopian brotherhood could look like, but throughout history there have been actual examples of TRUE manhood.

It is time for us to begin the Quest for TRUE manhood. We are needed in today's world. It is never too late to begin. Every breath you have left in this life can have TRUE value.

Do you practice ***TRUTHFULNESS****?*

Are you ***ROOTED*** *in your sense of self?*

Do you practice ***UNDERSTANDING*** *in your community?*

Do you want to live in a society that practices
ENLIGHTENED SELF-INTEREST*?*

These are the 4 Keys that will open the doorways to TRUE Manhood.

AS A SON, I wished for a father and elders who were TRUE.

AS A FATHER, I tried to practice TRUE manhood with my sons.

AS A TEACHER, I have taught these basic principles for decades.

AS A HUSBAND, I have been encouraged and challenged to live this code.

AS A MAN, I yearn and hope for a brotherhood of TRUE men.

To my friends of the Roundtable . . . I am saving you a seat.

WELCOME TO THE QUEST.

DO YOU KNOW YOUR "WHY?"

"This above all: to thine own self be true, and it must follow, as the night the day, Thou canst not then be false to any man."

~ William Shakespeare
Quote Hamlet Act 1, scene 3

Most of our daily thoughts and behaviors remain at the unconscious level and we rarely have time to question the way we live. We are bombarded with daily distractions and the WHY behind what we do slips in between the cracks of our very busy life. Most men do not spend conscious time decoding what is really valuable to them. We are too busy and distracted to consciously examine our motives and so we make many important decisions on auto-pilot. Advertisers and marketing companies already know this about us, and they create media content which reinforces us to remain unconscious.

The first step on your quest to Truth is to stop and really think about who you are and where you're going with your life. We call this Noble Question the "*Big Why*," and it is an essential part of what drives all of our actions, thoughts, and decisions.

Why we do the things we do.

Why we want the things we want.

Why we are driven (compelled) for success, marriage, or children.

What is your why?

Sometimes it's difficult to know how to make the best decisions in our life. We find ourselves struggling to choose between several alternatives. The answers may not seem clear to you at first, but by the time you are done with this process, you will have a better understanding of yourself and the direction you want to undergo. After completing this process, decision making and problem-solving will be aligned with your core principles.

Making important decisions in your life comes down to understanding what you value most in your Man Code. Often it's not the large decisions that determine your future but the smaller day-to-day decisions that have a greater long-term impact on your future. Once you know what's important to you, making decisions becomes a simple process.

What we hold as True in our belief system becomes a part of our daily thinking pattern, and over time that pattern creates our reality. Determining our own code of values (or ethics) will bring about the type of person each of us will become. You will notice an exponential increase in the amount of happiness, joy, and passion in your life.

And best of all, at the end of the process, you will know how to be True to yourself and to your own Man Code.

When we are true to ourselves, we become more authentic, confident and grounded, which in turn helps elevate the consciousness of the community.

Back to the story of Benjamin Franklin. At 27 he was working in a printing plant in Philadelphia yet he felt like he had not accomplished anything important with his life. He went through a bit of a mid-life crisis, and he began to ask himself these same types of Noble Questions that I am asking you.

Franklin discovered 13 values for himself, which he called the 13 Virtues in his autobiography. He then organized the rest of his life in accordance with these 13 values. He even organized his year into 13 week cycles and dedicated each cycle to focusing and writing on that one value. Over time, Franklin wrote that his values and his behavior eventually became congruous, and he felt a deep sense of inner peace living in alignment with his virtues.

As a result he contributed to the founding of America and he made his own life more productive in the process. Franklin became an extremely wealthy man and was able to retire in his forties--all by living according to those values that mattered to him the most.

In fact, this activity is how the founding fathers came together to create the new world known as America. They drafted a list of common values that they were seeking, and then they were able to create a government around that framework of values, which later became the Constitution.

On a personal level, we are each creating our own personal Constitution, or mission statement, which is our inner guide to all decisions that we make. Once we have completed this process for ourselves, we can extend this experience and create a set of shared values for our families, communities, and businesses. This activity can be healing for companies and corporations to help everyone on staff to know what the business values are. People are much more motivated to work for a code of values they can share in.

Most of us would not want to climb into a leaky boat and head out to the open ocean with no rudder, no engine, no oars, and no maps to guide us. Yet that is exactly how many of us make major decisions about our lives, and how we run our companies, our politics, and our economies. We end up feeling frustrated, scared, confused, and distrusting of our leadership—yet our leaders are also unsure without a proper rudder to guide them in the right direction. Your Man Code of values becomes your inner guidance system and allows you to become the Captain of your destiny.

"I am the master of my fate: I am the captain of my soul."

From Invictus by William Ernest Henley

CREATING YOUR OWN CODE OF VALUES

So where did we get the message(s) that told us what to value and what not to value? Where did these values come from? Most of us base our values on several sources:

Culture & Society (Society's Expectations)

Parental & Family Influences

Teachers & Authority Figures

Friends & Colleagues (The Need to Impress Others)

Media & Social Influences (Television, Movies, Internet)

Events & Experiences from Your Past (which leads to Fear of the Future)

Often our values were created in childhood and we tend to re-create a similar pattern in our own life as adults. If we create a life that is based on the value code of someone else, we will never be able to find our own happiness. We cannot put a puzzle together with someone else's puzzle pieces. It is like trying to operate a computer with the wrong source code. We will strive and struggle for success yet still feel empty at the end of the day. We will be exhausted from seeking approval in all the wrong places.

Imagine a man who has worked his whole life to climb the ladder of success only to find out that he has his ladder propped up against the wrong wall. Or a mountain climber who spends years getting to the pinnacle of the mountain only to find he was using the wrong map and he's climbed the wrong peak. Both men are successful at their task but they find themselves at an undesired and unintended destination.

But we can make our own personal code of values, our own **Man Code**, based on what we believe and what is TRUE for us. Finding out what is most important to you may seem like a daunting task at first. There are so many things to consider, but only one question really matters in this process:

What is most important to me in my life?

Below is a list of suggested values . . . intended as a guide to spark your own imagination. I encourage you to add your own ideas or concepts.

Write down 10 terms or concepts that you resonate strongly with and would like to have more of in your life.

_____

_____

_____

_____

_____

_____

_____

_____

_____

_____

Abundance, Accepting, Accomplishment, Achievement, Active Life, Admiration, Adventure, Advancement, Affection, Ambitious, Arts, Aspiring, Attractive, Authority, Autonomy, Balance, Beauty, Brave, Broad-minded, Brotherhood, Calmness, Capable, Challenge, Cheerful, Choice, Clean House, Comfort/Comfortable life, Competent, Commitment to Career, Companionship, Community, Communication, Confident, Conformity, Connection, Consistent, Contentedness, Contribution, Cooperation, Courage/Courageous, Courtesy, Creativity, Daring, Dependable, Decisive, Detachment, Determination, Discipline, Down to Earth, Drive, Dutiful, Education,

Effective, Equality/Equal opportunity, Enthusiastic, Entrepreneurship, Environment, Exciting life/Excitement, Fairness, Family (Connection with Family), Flexibility, Focused, Foodie, Forgiving, Freedom, Free from Pain, Free Time, Friendship, Frugal, Fun/Funny, Generous, Giving, Goofy, Grateful, Happy, Hard-working, Harmony (inner or outer), Having a Purpose, Healthy, Helpful, Honesty, Humble, Humor, Identity, Independence, Innovative, Integrity, Interaction with others, Intimacy, Imaginative, Insightful, Intellectual, Intelligent, Joyful, Justice, Kind, Knowledge, Leisurely life, Light-hearted, Listener, Logical, Love/Loving, Loyalty, Obedient, Open-minded, Optimistic, Organized, Organic, Mature, Mobility, Modesty, Motivated, Money, National Security, Nature, Nurturing, Partnership, Passion, Patient, Peace/Peaceful, Personal Growth, Personal Time, Playful, Pleasure, Polite, Popularity, Positive, Power, Practical, Preserving your Roots, Prosperous, Protective, Rational, Realistic, Reason, Recognition, Reflective, Relaxation, Reliable, Resilient, Respect/Respectful, Responsibility, Restrained, Safety, Security, Self-Controlled, Self-Directed, Self-Disciplined, Self-Esteem, Self-Less, Self-Reliant, Self-Respect, Self-Sufficient, Self-Worth, Sensitive, Serious, Sexual, Skilled, Sincere, Social Interest, Social Recognition, Speaking Your Truth, Spirituality, Spontaneity, Stability, Standing up for your Beliefs, Status, Stimulating, Strong, Success/Being Successful, Team-work, Tender, Thoughtful, Tolerance, Trusting, Truthful, Variety, Wealthy, Welfare of Others, Well-mannered, Wise (wisdom, an understanding of life), World Peace

PRIORITIZE YOUR MAN CODE

Now take the list of values and prioritize them in order of importance to you. The item that is most important goes at the top of the list. The next important goes next and so on with the entire list. Another way to organize your list is to try to shorten your list to only 5 and see which values come to the surface as being the most important that you absolutely could not do without.

Once you are clear about the order of your code of values, then no decision (big or small) will be difficult. From deciding whether or not to attend a party, to choosing your next career path, simply look at your Man Code of values and decide where your priorities are. Understanding your Man Code will help you recognize the areas of your life that need more attention, as well as what you want to prioritize in the future.

- For example, if you selected being a **Family Man** as one of your most important values, then you would not enjoy being in a job that takes you away from home for months at a time. You would probably prefer a job that allows you plenty of time for being at home—maybe even working from a home office.

- If **Loyalty** is one of your most important values, then you should not take a job that requires you to wine and dine other women when you are away from your wife.

- If **Freedom** is one of your most important values, then you may resent a job that clips your creative freedom no matter how much they pay you in salary.

- If you are a **Thrill-Seeking Risk Taker**, then you would probably not enjoy a career that involves sitting behind a desk in a safe job shuffling paperwork, but you might enjoy a career that requires you to travel to foreign countries and learn new languages.

When you identify and define your own Man Code, you can see the incongruence between what you want and what you have created. Knowing your values will also show you why you may be procrastinating or have poor motivation for an activity that is fairly low on your Man Code.

For instance, perhaps you value your **Health**, yet you have not been taking very good care of your body because you placed a higher value on your **Career**. Perhaps you want to quit smoking or you have been procrastinating about adding exercise to your routine in order to improve your current level of health and well-being. Let your code guide the actions that are needed for your life. If you see a place of your life where you are not living in alignment with your code, you can choose to make small positive steps in a new direction.

As the great Taoist philosopher Lao Tsu said, "A journey of 1000 miles begins with a single step."

How you prioritize your values is up to you. This must be your decision. The order of your values may also change as you go through

different stages of your life. We tend to crave more freedom as we are younger and then crave more security and stability as we get older . . . but every man is different. For instance, when you are young, unmarried, and in school, you may value college or training more than settling down with a family and taking on a mortgage. As you get older and you begin a family, your values may also change with you.

For many of us, our strongest values remain the same throughout our life. Often after you complete this process, you can look back at your childhood and see where you were living with or against your values and how you felt at that time. Perhaps you now know that you enjoy a great deal of privacy and quiet time, but you didn't know this about yourself in college. Maybe you exhausted yourself during those years as you tried to keep up with your pack of social college friends, because your values were different from theirs. If only we knew this information about our own Truth growing up. Can you imagine how much heartache and how many headaches we could have been spared?

There is a great cost to compromising our own Man Code. Most of the trouble that we get into in life comes about when we have forsaken our own value system—or placed a lower value item above a higher value item.

For example, let's take a man who values his freedom and passion for nature above security. This man agrees to take a full-time job that offers salary and security but allows him no free time for nature. He may enjoy the salary for a while but without any freedom or passion he will eventually feel depressed and withdrawn without knowing why. He might eventually feel as if he "*sold out*" because he made decisions that were in inverse order to his personal Man Code of values.

As men, if we are living in opposition to our own personal value system, we will feel uneasy and stressed. The more our behaviors and actions are out of line with our code of values, the more chaos and stress we will feel. This feeling of disquiet will soon become a simmering frustration and eventually can make us feel exhausted or quite ill. It is grueling to work against your Truth. When our actions are not in line with our code of values, then the natural emotional consequence is stress. Often we cope with this stress with unhealthy mechanisms such as excessive drinking, gambling or attempting to numb ourselves out. All we really need to do is to re-connect to who we are and the internal values that we cherish.

Often by the time we realize that we have been making decisions from the wrong source code, we experience what is known in the west as a mid-life crisis. We wake up one morning and wonder how we got to this point in our life. We try to change our ship's course midstream dragging wives, kids, and mortgages with us in our wake. When a man aimlessly wanders about not knowing where or how he fits in, he is likely to find despair, confusion, and unhappiness no matter what he attempts. This can be a time of deep trauma for a man who has never asked himself the Noble Questions, but you do not need to go down with the ship. There is another way.

Knowing what your values are and creating your own personal Man Code to live by those values is a powerful experience that will increase your confidence and inner peace. When we live by our code of values, we are less frustrated by the world. We begin to realize that we are not victims, or martyrs, or pack-mules burdened down by someone else's value system for us. We are free to create and choose and make mistakes and choose again.

Now imagine the man who places **Nurturing** and **Compassion** at the top of his value code. If he can find a career such as counseling, or volunteering in a hospice situation, he may find that his work days are aligned with his values.

When our actions are in line with our behavior, we will find a deeper sense of inner peace and contentment.

"Look at every path closely and deliberately, then ask ourselves this crucial question: Does this path have a heart? If it does, then the path is good. If it doesn't, it is of no use."

~ Carlos Castaneda

Each man's code will have some overlap but each will also be unique to your life experiences and desires. People who are not living according to their own value system or code, are apt to create more stress than is needed. But once you have clarified your own values and created your own Code, the process is organic and you will naturally experience more flow in your life. We feel more fulfilled and satisfied with ourselves when we enjoy the direction in which our life is going and we are certain about who we are. I offer you this invitation to welcome in more inner peace and happiness. Now you have your own Man Code of values. There is tremendous power in discovering and living according to our highest values.

I learned this, at least, by my experiment; that if one advances confidently in the direction of his dreams, and endeavors to live the life which he has imagined, he will meet with success in uncommon hours."

~ Henry David Thoreau

THE BRIDGE GAME

Here is a mental activity that will check whether you chose the most important values. All you will need to play the Bridge Game is your Imagination. Let's begin . . .

Let's say that you chose **Money & Prosperity** as one of your most important values. How much money will it take for you to feel successful?

Imagine that there is a short rope bridge stretched out a couple of feet across a tiny stream.

- Would you cross the rope bridge for $50?

- Would you cross the rope bridge for $500?

- Would you cross the rope bridge for $5000?

- Would you cross the rope bridge for $50,000?

- Would you cross the rope bridge for $500,000?

What would it take to change your decision? Would you cross the bridge for a better paying job? Would you cross the bridge for a lifetime of freedom? Would you cross the bridge to save a family member?

Now here is where your decisions really get real. Imagine that the rope bridge is now 100 feet long, and it is suspended between two cliff walls, thousands of feet in the air. At the bottom of the canyon is a raging, turbulent river that is moving in fast white-peaked torrents between jagged rocks. This time the bridge sways in the wind and shakes as you walk across it. Now let's see how you feel when your values and priorities are really put to the test.

- Would you cross the higher rope bridge for $50?

- Would you cross the rope bridge for $500?

- Would you cross the rope bridge for $5000?

- Would you cross the rope bridge for $50,000?

- Would you cross the rope bridge for $500,000?

What would it take to change your decision? Would you cross this higher, scarier, more dangerous bridge for a better paying job? Would you cross the bridge for a lifetime of freedom? Would you cross the bridge to save a family member? What if it was raining and the rope bridge became slippery? What do you value so much that you would be willing to risk your life?

ABOUT THE AUTHOR

KAI EHNES

Speaker, Author, Mentor

Kai was born in Germany and moved to America as a teenager. For over 25 years, Kai has also been an instructor and college professor of philosophy, psychology and economics. He has trained in Sustainability (EFS) at the Cloud Institute (NYC) and Systems Thinking through the Waters Foundation. As a keynote speaker and thought leader, Kai enjoys frequently addressing large audiences and he has been awarded the corporate speaker designation by the International Association of Corporate Speakers. Kai's vision is to inspire and ignite men to become authentic leaders in their community.

Website: www.kaiehnes.com

Email: kai@kaiehnes.com

ALSO BY KAI EHNES

- **Convene TRUE Men** - An interactive web application for TRUE men to share scenarios, offer their input, and create a New Man Code.

  http://convenecommunities.com/about-convene-true-men/

- **Your Action Plan to Unlock the Code to TRUE Manhood** - Please contact me for a FREE copy of this engaging self-assessment of your state of fulfillment.

  Contact: kai@kaiehnes.com

- **The Traveler's Song** - a musical journey to the notion of: "Go be true to yourself"

  https://itunes.apple.com/us/album/the-travelers-song/id694885522?i=694885576&ign-mpt=uo%3D4

www.ingramcontent.com/pod-product-compliance
Lightning Source LLC
Chambersburg PA
CBHW050821290526
45792CB00001B/216